the blue number counting book

with touch-sensitive numbers & illustrations

by Ellen C. Gould

design
Ellen C. Gould
artist
Cathy Kelly

Original © 1983 Learning Tools Company
Revised by Guy Campbell, 2001

ISBN # 978-0-938017-01-1

First printing 1983 • Reprint 2018

Printed in China

PARENT CHILD PRESS
BOOKS·ART

A division of Montessori Services
www.MontessoriServices.com

How to Use
the Blue Number
Counting Book

Teaching the Number Symbols.

1. **Show** the number shape, clearly **say** the name.

2. **Trace** the number with the right first finger and **say** the name again. (always start at the top)

3. **Guide** the child's finger to trace the number, **say** the name.

4. **Repeat**, using all the numbers.

Teaching the Number Quantity

1. **Read** the story, **point out** the colored areas of the pictures.

2. **Count out-loud** as you touch each area.

3. **Guide** the child's finger to touch each area, **count** with the child.

4. **Repeat** using different numbers.

Writing the Numbers

1. **Trace** the number shape with right first finger starting at the top.

2. **Copy** the number on chalk board or paper.

3. **Trace** and **Copy** each number many times.

One blanket for the baby.

2

Two goldfish swim in the water.

3 Three children
run with balloons.

4 Four kittens have blue ribbons.

5

Five ducklings
are at the pond.

6

Six flowerpots sit
on the steps.

7

Seven candles
shine on the
birthday cake.

8

Eight caterpillars
climb in the grass.

Nine clothes hang on the line.

10

Ten raindrops
fall into the
puddle.

0 Zero counts
nothing.